# ROYAL SCOT

## C.J. Freezer

*Foulis*

ISBN 0 85429 431 7

**A FOULIS Railway Book**

First published 1985
© **Winchmore Publishing
Services Ltd 1985**

Published by:
**Haynes Publishing Group**
Sparkford,
Yeovil,
Somerset BA22 7JJ

**Haynes Publications Inc.**
861 Lawrence Drive,
Newbury Park,
California 91320, USA

Produced by:
**Winchmore Publishing
Services Limited,**
40 Triton Square,
London NW1 3HG

Printed in England

Titles in the *Super Profile* series:

BSA Bantam (F333)
MV Agusta America (F334)
Norton Commando (F335)
Honda CB750 sohc (F351)
Sunbeam S7 & S8 (F363)
BMW R69 & R69S (F387)

Austin-Healey 'Frogeye'
Sprite (F343)
Ferrari 250GTO (F308)
Fiat X1/9 (F341)
Ford GT40 (F332)
Jaguar E-Type (F370)
Jaguar D-Type & XKSS (F371)
Jaguar Mk 2 Saloons (F307)
Lotus Elan (F330)
MGB (F305)
MG Midget & Austin-Healey Sprite
(except 'Frogeye') (F344)
Morris Minor & 1000 (ohv) (F331)
Porsche 911 Carrera (F311)
Triumph Stag (F342)

Avro Vulcan (F436)
B29 Superfortress (F339)
Boeing 707 (F356)
de Havilland Mosquito (F422)
Harrier (F357)
Mikoyan-Gurevich MiG 21 (F439)
P51 Mustang (F423)
Phantom II (F376)
Sea King (F377)
SEPECAT Jaguar (F438)
Super Etendard (F378)
Tiger Moth (F421)
Bell UH-1 Iroquois (F437)

Deltics (F430)
Great Western Kings (F426)
Green Arrow (F427)
Gresley Pacifics (F429)
InterCity 125 (F428)
Royal Scot (F431)

Library of Congress
Catalog Card Number
84-48789

Further titles in this series will be published at regular
intervals. For information on new titles please contact
your bookseller or write to the publisher.

Royal Scot super profile.——(Super profile)
  1. Locomotives——Great Britain
  I. Freezer, C.J.   II. Series
  625.2'61'0941    TJ603.4.G7

# Contents

Small Engines                              4

Locomotive Exchanges                       9

Seeking a Design                          12

The First Royal Scots                     14

Scots in Service                          25

Fury                                      27

Stanier and the LMS                       31

The Rebuilt Scots                         34

The Final Years                           37

What's in a Name                          45

Modelling Notes                           51

Specifications                            55

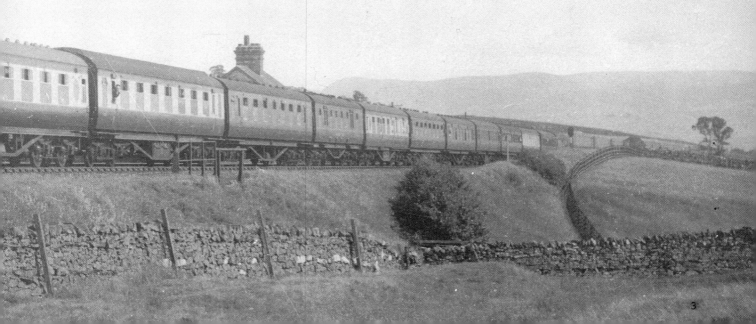

# Small Engines

Everyone who has ever taken the slightest interest in British railways will have heard of the *Royal Scot*. For some, it will be *the* train that immediately springs to mind, a train that leaves Euston at 10:00 am and arrives at Glasgow Central a little over five hours later. Today the train is electrically hauled by a powerful class 87 BoBo locomotive. The heavy load, made up entirely of the latest Mk III air conditioned coaches, is pulled over the summits at Shap and Beattock with an ease which is both amazing and anticlimatic to those who knew the route in the Steam Age.

The train was steam-hauled at the outset. Initially, not only were the locomotives exchanged at Carlisle, but the train itself was almost invariably double-headed. The locomotive exchange at Carlisle had been a feature of West Coast operation from the inception of the service, for it was then a frontier station. Indeed, in pre-group days Carlisle Citadel was one of the most fascinating stations in Britain, with locomotives and trains from no less than six companies, four English and two Scottish, sharing the rails. But, for the predominant West Coast route, it marked the end northward of LNWR rails and the start of the Caledonian Railway.

In 1923, all this was swept away. Just two railways used the station and the London, Midland and Scottish Railway, the largest in Britain – and one of the largest in the world – was the dominant force.

On the formation of the LMS railway, command of the locomotive stock was initially handed to the senior CME of one of the constituent companies, George Hughes of the Lancashire & Yorkshire Railway, which had amalgamated with the LNWR one year earlier. There is little doubt that the choice was a mistake, as Hughes was nearing retirement. However, he did bring out one highly successful locomotive design, the 5P5F 'Crab' 2-6-0, although this was not to appear until after his resignation. It was an ungainly but useful beast, destined to last almost to the end of steam, outliving many later productions. He also introduced to the main routes his four-cylinder 4-6-0, which was not a striking success.

Indeed, no existing express passenger class on the new railway could be regarded as a good example of modern steam locomotive practice. The LNWR, Caledonian, Lancashire and Yorkshire, and Glasgow and South Western had all been unsuccessful in producing a 4-6-0 that was both powerful and free-running. As for the Midland, it never even tried, believing that small engines were best. A railway alphabet of pre-1914 vintage is memorable for one couplet:

> M is for Midland, with engines galore,
> They've two on each train,
> Yet they hanker for more.

This was not so much libellous as verging on the truth. Double-heading was a way of life on the Midland as the LNWR had never shaken off the effects of the draconian limits imposed on the Webb Compounds, and these had led to a lot of double-heading on its trains.

But to be fair, the Midland

Preserved No 6115.

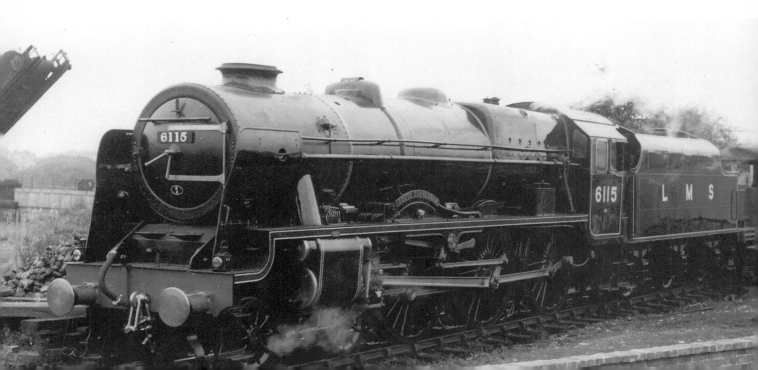

regarded itself as a successful and competitive line. It had extended to London rather than moved out from the Capital and with a good secure revenue based on coal traffic it was in a position to offer patrons a superior service. In this connection it is worth recalling that the present relief lines on the electrified route to Bedford were originally reserved solely for freight, and were better graded than the main line, such was the importance of coal traffic in the Midland's economy.

The Midland also abolished third class and gave all second class passengers soft seats, initiating the British practice of providing considerable comfort for all passengers. On entering a British second class saloon, visiting continental travellers have been known to go back outside to check if they've not drifted into the first class by mistake. The Midland also believed in a frequent service of fast, light trains, another great boon to the passenger.

The LNWR believed in an equally frequent service but as befitted the first northern route out of London, and one of the busiest, they needed somewhat heavier trains.

All would have been well but for the fact that traffic control on the new railway fell into the hands of James Anderson, a Midland man. The Midland traffic organisation, with the possible exception of the Great Eastern, had previously been better than any other in Britain. James Anderson was a sound man when it came to organising the routeing of trains, the best and most economical use of stock, and the arrangement of a timetable that went as far as was commercially possible towards meeting the needs of the travelling public. Unfortunately, he was also a firm believer in the small engine policy and as ex-head of the Derby drawing office, he had very clear ideas on locomotive design. These revolved around one simple dictum: the standards laid down

by Derby around the turn of the century were as near to perfection as is possible. It is odd to realise that a man whose main work lay in organising traffic, had a blind spot on bearing sizes. A lot of the trouble on the LMS arose because driving axleboxes designed for a class three locomotive were fitted to more powerful machines, and produced a rash of hot boxes.

At this point it is difficult to say just how far Anderson influenced affairs and how much of the detail stagnation that followed was due to the fact that Derby design had become too well organised and highly resistant to change. One thing however is clear. Not only did the LMS settle on the somewhat underpowered 4P Compound 4-4-0 as its principal new express locomotive, but the even less effective 2P 4-4-0 was also made an LMS standard. In the latter case, the tiny locomotives proved useful on secondary routes, even if they had to work in tandem on the Somerset & Dorset joint lines.

It is certain that none of this would have happened had it not been for the next CME of the LMS, Sir Henry Fowler. He was in many ways an admirable man, and an excellent engineer, but somewhat disinterested in locomotive design. Once, in a jovial mood, he slapped a friend on the back and said, 'My dear fellow, I never designed a locomotive in my life'.

Not that this was really unusual. Although it was customary to attribute the design of locomotives to the man who held office, either as Locomotive Superintendant or later, as Chief Mechanical Engineer, in practice not all have done more than sign the drawings presented to them. Fowler's preference for other aspects of his post eventually proved to be a bad thing. He had at his command a very sound design team and it appears that generally he allowed the drawing office to initiate designs. Had there been a senior draughtsman with radical ideas all

would have been well, but unfortunately, the most influential man with ideas on locomotive design, Anderson, tended to hark back to the successful past. So the LMS produced a large number of compounds which rapidly spread over the system. In their bright red livery they were soon dubbed 'Crimson Ramblers', but as a suitable head for a major West Coast express they lacked a vital ingredient – tractive effort! In every other respect the compounds were magnificent machines, – with suitable loads and in the hands of sympathetic enginemen, they performed prodigies of work. Unfortunately, there remained on the LNWR several firm convictions based on experiences with the Webb designs; compounds could not run fast, nor could Derby produce a good locomotive. Even on a bad day, a compound was as useful as the magnificent looking but ineffectual Claughton four-cylinder 4-6-0, and the antiquated inside cylindered 4-6-0s of the 'Prince of Wales' and 'Experiment' classes. The situation on the West Coast route was ridiculous and double-heading became the norm.

To be absolutely fair, plenty of locomotive men were aware that things could be better. They had only to look at the other three companies to see this was so. It was clear that, although some parts of the locomotive and traffic department were perfectly happy to let things continue in the way they were, there were those with ideas for future locomotives.

One was H.M. Beames, of Crewe. If any man on the new railway had cause to complain against fate, it was he. In line for the prestigious post of CME of the LNWR, he saw it snatched away. Left in charge of the works, he produced a tank version of the Super D 0-8-0, an effective looking 0-8-4 side tank locomotive. Whilst not a failure, it was hardly a success because the LNWR had little use for such a machine

5

## L.M.S.R. Royal Scot
## Locomotive Class 6P
## Key to Items

 1  Chimney
 2  Steam Collector Dome
 3  Ross 'Pop' Safety Valves
 4  Boiler Casing
 5  Steam Pipes
 6  Superheater Header
 7  Fire Tubes
 8  Superheater Tubes
 9  Superheater Elements
10  Blast Pipe
11  Petticoat Pipe
12  Smokebox
13  Smokebox Door
14  Piston Valves
15  Inner Cylinder
16  Buffers
17  Coupling Hook
18  Bogie
19  Piston Rod
20  Slide Bar

21  Connecting Rod
22  Combination Lever
23  Crank Arm Balance Weight
24  Driving Wheels
25  Springs
26  Brake Cylinder
27  Brake Rods
28  Coupling Rod
29  Firebox
30  Whistle
31  Reversing Rod
32  Firebars
33  Ashpan
34  Driving Cab
35  Vacuum Brake Connection
36  Main Frame
37  Sand Pipes
38  Lamp Brackets
39  Handrail
40  Guard Irons

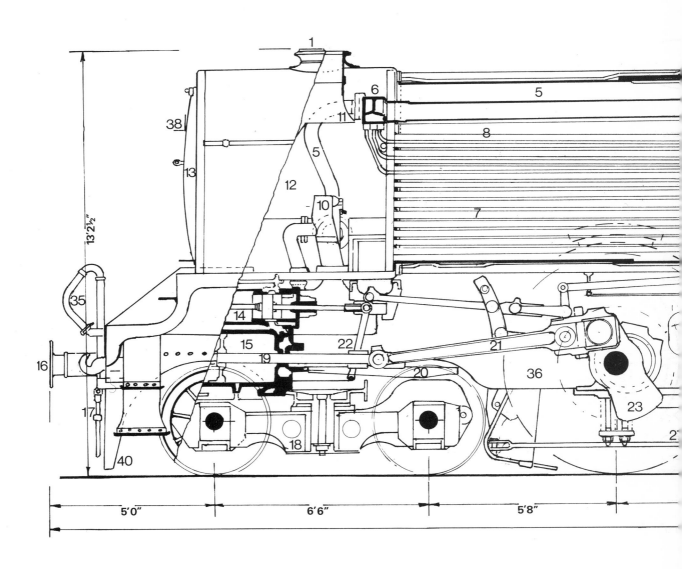

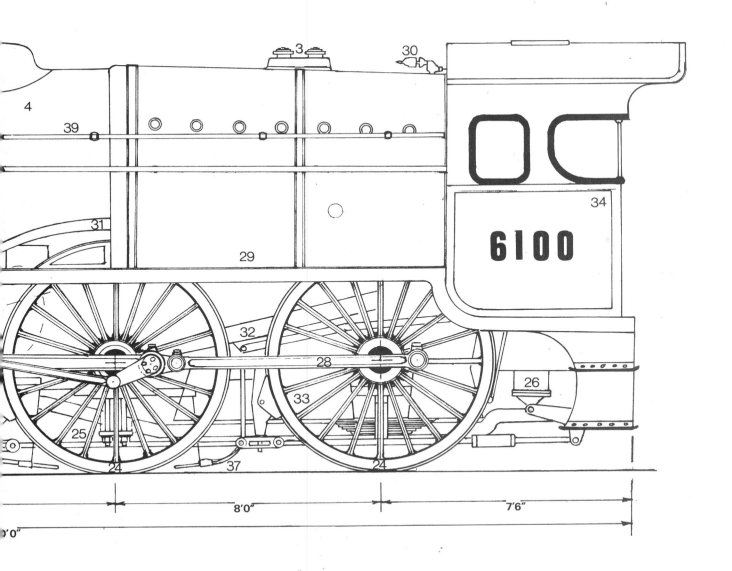

3

30

4

39

31

29

34

6100

32

28

26

33

25

24

37

24

8'0"

7'6"

0'0"

outside the Welsh valleys.

He also improved the Prince of Wales 4-6-0s, probably the best large locomotive the LMS possessed. Their weakness was inside the Joy's valve gear, which involved a joint in the connecting rod, causing problems on high powered locomotives. Beames' solution was an odd form of Walschaerts gear, mounted outside and driving the inside valves through rocker arms. The whole arrangement looked decidedly peculiar, and the locomotives so fitted were nicknamed 'Tishys' after a racehorse that crossed its front legs during the Derby. Although the 'Tishys' ran well, an improved design of connecting rod eventually solved the difficulty in a more elegant fashion.

Beames had something of an obsession with inside cylinders, for he was involved in a later scheme for a mixed traffic 4-6-0, with inside cylinders and high running boards.

Meanwhile there were fresh ideas floating around Derby. Although the Smith-Deely-Fowler compound 4-4-0s were excellent machines and highly economical, they were small and lacked punch. That the compound arrangement worked well was without question. The Smith system was one of the tiny handful of fundamentally sound compound locomotives produced, and with the Deely improvements, in particular the ingenious regulator that allowed simple and semi-compound working to be arranged without a mass of complicated controls, they proved a good driver's machine.

The design was basically a turn of the century machine with short travel valves and had only been modified slightly by the provision of superheat and slightly smaller drivers. It was clear that with better valve events and a modern front end, they could easily be improved.

The first proposal was for a three-cylinder compound 4-6-0, basically an enlarged 4P 4-4-0. In a way, it was rather a pity that this line was not pursued. Instead, more grandiose schemes for a four-cylinder 4-6-2 were favoured. The second proposal reached the point of authorisation and it seems that material was ordered and the frames laid out in Derby works.

When one studies the drawings, it is clear that Derby had to a certain extent, taken heed of what was happening elsewhere and were anxious to produce a really large locomotive. Much would have depended on which half of the Derby office drew up the cylinders and valve gear. In the superb 2-6-4 tanks, a thoroughly modern front end produced a locomotive that performed well. With an enthusiastic crew and a clear road, it was capable of speeds in the high eighties, whereas the almost contemporary 2-6-2 tanks had an ungainly front end and had difficulties hauling a four coach train.

'George Hughes', L & Y R 4-6-0 No 1674, on down Scotch Express near Harrow in 1924. A LNWR 12-wheel composite coach is next to the locomotive.

# Locomotive Exchanges

In 1926, the LMS locomotive department seemed cosy enough. However, enthusiasts were divided as to its merits, depending on whether one preferred Crewe to Derby. If one preferred Derby then all was well as the present policy proved that the Midland was right. If one preferred Crewe, or for that matter Cowlairs, then things were not quite so good. Nevertheless as the 'Claughtons' and 'Cardeans' were still in evidence, even though they were painted a horrid scarlet, matters were still tolerable.

On the railway itself, things were less promising. In his autobiography E.S. Cox describes how the younger men in the design office were far from happy with the way things were going, especially as events in Wiltshire were proving a fine example.

The GWR had taken the highly successful four-cylinder 'Star' 4-6-

Royal Scot No. 46149 built as *The Lady of the Lake* in 1927 and later renamed *The Middlesex Regiment.*

0 chassis and fitted a larger boiler and larger cylinders. The result was the 'Castle', arguably the best all round four-cylinder 4-6-0 ever built. It was fast, it hauled heavy trains and above all, it returned figures for coal consumption that were unbelievable.

Meanwhile the LMS Board were not altogether pleased with their current arrangements. Unlike Mr Anderson, they probably felt that two locomotives, with two crews, and two tenders full of coal on every important train was not the best way to run a railway. They may also have had a sneaking feeling that the new company was doing its level best to live up to its scurrilous nickname, the 'Ell of a Mess railway!

So, in 1925, a locomotive exchange was arranged with the GWR and the 5000 *Launceston Castle* was sent onto the West Coast route to be tried in service. This was not the first time a GWR 4-6-0 had run over the West Coast route. In 1910 *Polar Star* had shown her paces and had been far

better at hauling the trains on the LNWR than the 'Experiment' class *Worcestershire* had been at handling the GWR traffic. Unfortunately, no-one on the LNWR seems to have impressed on the shed foreman that the Company's reputation was at stake: and so he sent the locomotive he could best spare. *Worcestershire* was by no means a good example of the class and so, to a degree, the results were inconclusive, but the LNWR were sufficiently impressed with the *Star* to build a class of four-cylinder locomotives. Although the result was extremely elegant, the Claughtons were not particularly distinguished performers and on the whole, ushered in a period of indifferent design at Crewe that continued until the grouping.

The 1926 exchange followed hard on the heels of the 1925 contest. Generally, the 1925 trials served to show that the long travel valves fitted to the 'Castle' were preferable to the old-fashioned short travel valves of the Gresley Pacific, and the development of the A3 'Super Pacific' followed. In other words, the exchanges demonstrated that a particular

arrangement, still rather controversial, was definitely superior, and as a result, nearly all future British steam locomotive designs received better front ends. In fact, the exchange between the LNER and the GWR was a serious experiment which had only been turned into a contest by astute publicists.

Once again the LMS agreed to an interchange and the Paddington Publicity machine prepared itself for the fray. Everyone thought that it would be another close contest for the Claughtons had, after all, been developed after Crewe had had a good look at a 'Star', and although it was a matter of pride for Swindon men to deride the other works, no engineer of any ability would seriously suggest that either Crewe or Derby were incompetent. Everyone was in for a surprise.

This time the results of the locomotive exchange were clear cut and unchallenged. Without

exaggeration the Castle outshone everything that the LMS could offer. It was not strictly speaking a fair exchange for the LMS borrowed a Castle and in turn sent the GWR a compound. The small 4-4-0 was eventually returned to the LMS with the conventional polite comments. These, as E.L. Ahrons pointed out usually ran something like this; 'It's a nice machine, beautifully built, easy to handle, and your men performed well on a strange road. However, there is something about the alignment of our line that doesn't quite suit it.'.

By no stretch of the imagination could anything like that be said about the performance of *Launceton Castle.* The loan lasted for five weeks, and the locomotive was stationed at Crewe. For the first fortnight the engine worked between Crewe and Euston, beginning with moderately heavy trains, and then moving forward to a gross tonnage in excess of 500

(508 tonnes). Then it was the turn of the Crewe-Carlisle run.

The southern section of the LNWR is easily graded, and although it never achieved the near-level alignment that Brunel produced, it had no severe banks. Between Crewe and Lancaster the gradients were also reasonable but then began the notorious climb up to Shap summit. Banking was normal over this section. Therein lay the fundamental difference in outlook between Crewe and Swindon. Under Churchward, double-heading, even over the notorious South Devon banks was frowned upon, and so Shap was tackled unassisted.

Fortunately, Cecil J. Allen was on hand to take notes and has set them out in his book *The Locomotive Exchanges.* It is not therefore necessary to go into great detail, since anyone fascinated by locomotive logs can refer to this book. He describes how, even with loads in excess of 400 tons (406 tonnes), *Launceston Castle* with Driver Young at the controls, was in complete mastery of the load, and kept time with ease. This mastery was demonstrated a few days later when, on a blustery day, the antique gravity sanding gear favoured by the GWR proved more ineffectual than usual. On the exposed stretches of the line beyond Preston, the locomotive began to slip, loosing a fair amount of time in the process. However, as soon as more sheltered sections were reached and the sanding gear became reasonably effective, time was made up, and but for a signal check at Penrith, the run would have been slightly ahead of schedule at Carlisle.

The contrast between every item of motive power on the LMS and the GWR was too marked not to be noticed. Even Paddington decided that to put this forward as a contest would be in bad taste. It was obvious that the GWR's Castle was a locomotive capable of pulling any contemporary train in Britain. That it wouldn't go through the tunnels on most of the lines was only a minor detail that pedants could argue about!

The LMS board was suitably impressed. Plans were afoot to start a new train the following year, and the name had already been chosen, 'The Royal Scot'. The loan of the Castle had shown that there was nothing about the West Coast route that made it imperative to resort to double heading. Not only could one locomotive run from Euston to Carlisle but, unless the train was exceptionally heavy, it needed no assistance to tackle either Shap or Beattock.

At this point it is worth mentioning what was surely the finest fling of an LMS compound. In 1927 the LNER announced the institution of non-stop services from Kings Cross to Edinburgh Waverley. Possibly the new LMS train had some bearing on this decision, and the Gresley corridor tender was built so that crews could be exchanged en route.

The practical value of a non-stop run of this magnitude was arguable, but in the 1920s there were other good reasons for such a move. A great deal of passenger traffic was still rail bourne, and although private cars were growing in numbers and in reliability, the greater comfort of the express train was still an important factor. Between stops one remained undisturbed and so a non-stop run had its attractions, providing sufficient demand was available to produce a decent loading. In the 1920s, railways made good newspaper copy, and the longest non-stop run in the world was certain to get a good many column inches in the papers. This gave the LNER useful free advertising and with a large stock of powerful modern locomotives, they were in a good position to exploit any increase in popularity.

The overall speed of the non-stop train was only marginally higher than that of the normal stopping service. But this was immaterial, as the effect was primarily psychological, a point the LNER public relations office fully appreciated.

There is no doubt that the announcement of a non-stop run from Kings Cross to Edinburgh was calculated to annoy the LMS, as well as persuade some travellers to think of a different route to Scotland. Although Kings Cross served Edinburgh and Euston ran to Glasgow, for anyone heading to the Highlands, either route made an equally good start to the long and tiring journey.

Competition between the rival lines to Scotland had been more or less at a standstill for decades. Both schedules and fares had been pegged to prevent a recurrence of the exciting, but commercially dubious 'Races to the North'. But by the 1920's rivalry between the railways was largely cosmetic. The grouping had effectively wiped out local competition, with each of the 'Big Four' having a virtual railway monopoly within its territory.

The LMS were certainly goaded, and retaliated. One day before the LNER non-stop service started they made a slight modification to the working of the Royal Scot. This train normally divided at Carlisle, one portion going to Edinburgh whilst the other, larger section ran to Glasgow. On the 27 April 1927, the train was run in two parts, the light Edinburgh section being headed by compound No 1054. With a fairly light load and an expert crew it made it – but only just. There was less than a hundredweight of coal left in the tender, and just enough steam to reach the shed. It was of course a stunt, but it was regarded as a particularly good one.

However, this was of little use to the operating department. Although the Royal Scot was, from the outset, booked to run non-stop to Carlisle, in fact it came to a halt outside Carnforth to exchange locomotives. This was only a stop-gap solution as the Castle had shown that something better was possible. The board issued a veiled ultimatum to the CME – produce a modern locomotive that will do the work of a Castle on the LMS – or else!

It is clear that Anderson had little faith in the Compound Pacific, and equally clear that he had sufficient influence to put his ideas into practice. Work stopped on the Compound Pacific; Sir Henry Fowler's masterpiece was never to appear. This, more than anything else, showed that he was not joking when he disclaimed responsibility for locomotive design. Such an order, to a CME who cared deeply about new designs, would have been seen as an invitation to resign and other men have done as much.

# Seeking a Design

It was easy enough for the Board to tell the locomotive department to produce a new locomotive. Authority to spend the necessary capital was given, and there ended the straightforward part of the job. Indeed, there is a persistent story to the effect that some members of the board, realising the difficulties wished to order 50 Castles from the GWR.

It is an interesting tale but there are very good reasons why it is at best, nothing more than an echo of earlier discussions on the subject. In the wake of the loan, it could have been a jocular suggestion made by one of the Board without any thought as to its practicality. At worst, it is a pure fabrication, for there were two distinct snags.

The first was the loading gauge. As a result of Brunel's forethought, the GWR had the most generous loading gauge in Britain. Although this mainly arose from his adoption of the broad gauge, it is not generally appreciated that Brunel grasped at the very outset the importance of the loading gauge, and established a standard width and height for his trains. This contrasted favourably with the engineers of the Stephenson school, who stuck to the one gauge, and often, especially in the early years, left very tight spots on their lines at places where it would be both difficult and costly to open them out – Tylers Hill Tunnel on the Canterbury and Whitstable was not the only example of this particular error. So, as a result, GWR four-cylinder locomotives could only run over limited stretches of foreign rails, and 50 Castles would have created havoc on the LMS, carving platforms to the right and left of them as they hacked their way through routes never built for so wide a machine.

There was, however, a more significant obstacle. Many years before, Crewe had contracted to build a number of locomotives for the Lancashire & Yorkshire Railway. It was an excellent arrangement for the two companies had long worked in harmony. However, it was not viewed in a similar spirit by the British locomotive manufacturers who considered their legitimate business interests were under threat. They lobbied Parliament with considerable effect and as a result the LNWR were prevented from contracting to build any more locomotives for other users. The ban on railway workshops competing for business remained in force until the 1960s, when the works were hived off into a quasi independent organisation, able to compete for work outside the confines of the nationalised system. As this ban was not a great secret it is unlikely that the LMS board would have ever seriously considered the possibility of ordering locomotives from the GWR.

Yet, there is no doubt that someone on the LMS, possibly the design office, possibly the board acting independently, sent a request to the GWR for a set of working drawings of the Castle. The request was politely refused, although it is difficult to see why. After all *Launceston Castle* had been at Crewe for five weeks and there could have been few secrets left. Possibly there was some feeling that a commercial design was a valuable property, but this could have been met by sending a pro-forma invoice. However, it is more likely that the GWR felt that, as the LMS had already used the locomotive for over a month, if they had not taken enough data to give details to their drawing office then they had wasted a glorious opportunity!

However, the Southern were more amenable and a complete set of drawings of the new 4-6-0 'Lord Nelson' class was despatched to Derby, with Mr Maunsell's compliments. Not that Derby did a great deal with them. It seems obvious today that someone on the LMS had a fairly clear idea about the new locomotive design – and it wasn't Sir Henry Fowler!

John Anderson has often been put forward as the eminence gris in the new company. A lot of this is due to the slant given to the events by E.S. Cox, who, as one of the bright young designers of the new company, seems to have resented the fact that someone outside the drawing office could influence locomotive design. Anderson did not like the compounds nor did he want a Pacific. His attitude was consistent and straight-forward – use the least parts that you can. Anderson wanted a three-cylinder 4-6-0 and he got it.

With hindsight, it is odd that Derby did not dig in its heels and finish the Compound Pacifics. After all, the design was already worked out; there had been some work done on the first two, and, given a little determination they could have completed initial running-in tests in good time for the new service. There must have been some rather nasty goings on in the corridors of Euston around that time.

Instead, the LMS tacitly admitted that it could not build the locomotives in time. The job was farmed out to the North British Locomotive Works in Glasgow, who then worked in close consultation with the design team at Derby. What is more, 50 locomotives were ordered off the drawing board.

This was generally described as an extreme gamble, but it was not quite so big a leap in the dark as it seemed. The explanation lies in the underlying difference between the railway workshops and the commercial locomotive builders of Britain.

In the heyday of steam, the works had a more important function than just the construction of locomotives. Their main purpose was to maintain the existing stock in good order, and to overhaul every other piece of machinery owned by the company. In order to perform this efficiently and rapidly, it was essential to provide all the machinery and plant needed to make any part. Consequently, it was easy enough to construct locomotives 'in house', and since this made sense to the enquiring shareholder, it was encouraged. In practice, cost and time were secondary considerations and there is a distinct possibility that not all the overheads were included in the price given in the company's accounts.

On occasions, railway workshops could turn out a locomotive quickly – for example

Swindon produced the first 'King' in time for the Baltimore & Ohio Centenary celebrations. In general, however, new locomotives were designed and built at a comparatively leisurely pace and it was usually possible to construct a prototype and arrange extended trials whenever a radical departure from accepted practice was envisaged. This is a simple example of treating engineering as a fine art. Even when a class was ordered it was normally built in small batches, and detail changes often took place as successive lots went through the works.

The commercial locomotive builders had a totally different approach. For instance, they found it essential to keep costs low since building could not be cross subsidised by repairs or maintenance. It was equally essential to produce completely reliable machines. During the twentieth century, a lot of the business of the larger works, such as the North British Locomotive Company, was concentrated on

overseas orders. Although the new locomotive was a big one for the LMS, it was nothing out of the ordinary for the North British. They had been making successful locomotives of this size and power rating for decades.

Indeed, it is probable that the design was farmed out because it was feared that such a pressure project would throw Derby and Crewe into complete confusion, whereas the North British designers, foremen and craftsmen considered an urgent order to be all in a day's work.

It was a considerable achievement to take on the job of producing 50 prestige locomotives under pressure. It was however, exactly the sort of challenge that any of the larger British locomotive manufacturers relished, and upon which their reputation was based. It was British commercial engineering at its incomparable best. The job was handed out in the full knowledge that it would not only be done on time, but also in style and with complete success.

In original form, No 6137 as built for the LMS by North British Locomotive at their Hyde Park Works, here shown near Camden Shed with Chalk Farm Station in the background. It was later renamed *The Prince of Wales' Volunteers*.

# The First Royal Scots

The design of the Royal Scots was as original as any British 4-6-0 could be in the 1920s. The impetus came from the successful work of *Launceston Castle* and certainly the *Lord Nelson* drawings proved of interest. However the Scots had little in common with the Nelsons apart from an identical wheel formula and a similar outline at the firebox.

The coupled wheelbase broke firmly with Derby tradition. In place of the almost inevitable 8ft + 8ft 6in (2.4 m + 2.6 m) division that had been a Derby standard ever since mid Victorian years when a jig had been built to ensure reasonably accurate alignment of the hornblocks, the driving wheels were now spaced at 7ft 4in + 8ft (2.2 m + 2.4 m). Again this differed from the Nelson spacing of 7ft +

8ft (2.1 m + 2.4 m). The relatively close spacing of the last pairs of wheels led to the adoption of a stepped grate, here there was a similarity with the Nelsons, but then, quite a few 4-6-0s had this particular feature. Few were quite so successful.

Three-cylinder simple expansion with divided drive was adopted. The single inside cylinder drove the leading axle whilst the outside pair drove the centre wheels with three independant sets of Walschaerts valve gear. Here was a definite difference between the Royal Scots and all other contemporary British locomotives, and an arrangement that met the requirements admirably. The practical advantages were considerable, although on paper the

reciprocating balance was less effective than with a four-cylinder drive, or a three-cylinder machine with all engines driving one axle, as in the Gresley designs. As long travel piston valves were fitted at the outset, the locomotive was both efficient and free running.

The boiler had a very large barrel for the period, a feature that was accentuated by the Derby design team's insistence on the old style flanged smokebox rather than the more modern drumhead pattern. There was some doubt as to the ability to maintain a tight joint here, although this type of smokebox had been successfully used elsewhere in Britain for over 30 years.

One consequence of this choice of design was that the clearance between the top of the smokebox and the loading gauge was

No 6147 *Courier* approaching Watford Junction with a local electric to Watford on the right-hand side.

extremely limited and the chimney had to be very squat, a matter of 7$\frac{7}{16}$ inches (19 cm). As the chimney was of normal diameter, the result was either impressive or faintly ludicrous, depending upon your point of view. The writer has always felt that a wider false casing would have been more aesthetically pleasing although the actual working part proved correct within the tenets of the period. It would be pleasant to imagine a Lemaitre or Kylchap chimney, but one could hardly expect the North British Locomotive Co to anticipate events! One can perhaps be thankful that no-one was tempted to fit a simple stovepipe; that would have been the crowning insult.

The belpaire firebox differed appreciably from both the Castle and Lord Nelson designs, which incorporated highly sophisticated tapered and curved sides. The Scot pattern was square and forthright, a rather retrograde step on paper, though it performed perfectly well in service.

The boiler pressure of 250 psi (17 bar) was high by LMS standards, but was in keeping with contemporary practice. Maintenance problems increased with the higher pressures, but this was not a serious worry compared to the greater power derived. At high pressure there is a slight theoretical increase in thermal efficiency, but it is unlikely that this had any great bearing in practice. From the outset, high superheat was adopted.

The leading bogie was equalised, with a wheelbase of 6ft 6inches (2.0 m) and 10 spoked 3ft 3½inches (0.99 m) diameter wheels. The driving wheels, of 6ft 9inches (2.06 m) diameter had 21 spokes. This was a fairly conventional set of sizes for an express passenger locomotive. At that time, it was considered obvious that the largest possible driving wheels permitted the highest speeds. The maximum axle load was 20 ton 18 cwt (21236

kg), which, because of the very low hammerblow, due to the better balanced three-cylinder drive, was acceptable to the civil engineers.

The new locomotive appeared very impressive despite its standard Derby 3,500 gallon (15,911 l) tender, which came as something of an anticlimax. But to be fair, the GWR were still turning out Castles with a similar style tender and only the LNER and Southern were equipping their newer, large locomotives with high capacity tenders.

The detail design work was undertaken by the North British Locomotive Co., creating a great deal of overtime work in the already fully occupied drawing office. The design was clearly influenced by Derby and Herbert Chambers, their chief draughtsman, spent two days in Glasgow every fortnight seeing that Derby's ideas were incorporated. Sir Henry Fowler's involvement in the new locomotives only amounted to signing the drawings.

The construction of 50 large locomotives in short order taxed the resources of the North British Locomotive Co to the limit. One of the company's three works had been closed, and so the order was split, 25 engines were built at the former Dubs works at Queen's Park and another 25 at the former Neilson Reid works at Springburn. Although both works were eventually owned by the one conglomerate, traditions died hard. Whilst the Neilson 25 received round works plates, the 'Dubs' batch had the traditional diamond shaped pattern.

Running numbers 6100-24 were allocated to the Queen's Park machines, 6125-49 going to Hyde Park. However, Hyde Park were the first to complete a locomotive, and so 6125 was finished in the usual photogenic grey livery and temporarily numbered 6100 for the prestige photo. Needless to say, the works plate is a complete give-away on the official picture.

Early photographic plates were completely colour blind, for example red appeared as if it was black. Consequently the practice arose of photographing the locomotive in a grey undercoat and adding, usually in white water-based paint, the lining and lettering with only the black portions in their correct colour. The result was a locomotive that appeared correct in a black-and-white photograph. Modelmakers should treat official photographs of steam locomotives as unreliable guides for painting, for it is by no means certain that the lining is correct either!

It would be pleasant to record that North British made a profit out of the deal, but in fact the total contract price was £386,250 whilst the cost on the books was set at £285,236.13s.11d.

6100 was named *Royal Scot,* and the first 25 locomotives were similarly named after regiments. The last batch carried names which had been given to early locomotives on the LMS constituents and a brass plate with an engraved elevation of the locomotive was added to the centre splasher. The locomotives were delivered between July and November 1927. At long last, the LMS had an express passenger locomotive worthy of the world's largest railway.

In accordance with long standing custom, the new locomotives were attributed to Sir Henry Fowler. Few knowledgeable engineers of the time believed this, and today most locomotive enthusiasts are aware of his complete disinterest in the evolution of these machines. Nevertheless, credit went to Henry Fowler although it is doubtful if he ever appreciated the fact. He was an honourable man and had the design been less than successful, he would have taken the blame — among other things, that was what he was paid for.

The down 'Royal Scot' hauled by No 6138
*Fury* in 1928.

No 6115 'Scots Guardsman', having just left New Mills tunnel

*Above*: Royal Scot No 46142 'The York & Lancaster Regiment' takes a light load through the Lune Valley in June 1963.

In 1953 'Royal Horse Guardsman', No 46151, at Bay Horse with a train to Windermere.

*Above*: 'The North Staffordshire Regiment', No 46141, works hard to get a freight away from Oxenholme in June 1963.

In September 1964 'Kings Royal Rifle Corps, No 46140, crosses the Clyde at Crawford.

*Above*: Rebuilt Scot No 46118 'Royal Welch Fusilier' climbs past Shap Wells with a down express in August 1963.

*Inset*: No 46148 'The Manchester Regiment' in July 1962 passes Lancaster with the down Lakes Express.

*Below*: Passing Howgill in August 1962, 7P No 46108 'Seaforth Highlander' brings a Manchester train from Aberdeen.

*Above*: 'Royal Scot' No 6100 (actually No 6152) prepared for its visit to the Chicago World's Fair in 1933 in original livery.

'The Middlesex Regiment', 6P No 6149, at Crewe in April 1937, in original LMS livery.

*Above*: A stormy May evening in 1959 and No 46166 'London Rifle Brigade' brings a down express to Perth preparatory to handing over to No 44997.

Still in original build though in BR black, No 46163 'Civil Service Rifleman' at Rugby shed in May 1953.

*Right*: Although classified 7P No 46162, 'Queens Westminster Rifleman' hauls a freight train for Carlisle through the Lune Valley in June 1963.

Fitted with straight BR-pattern smoke deflectors, No 46106 'Gordon Highlander' picks up water on Castlethorpe Troughs near Wolverton in 1958.

*Above*: On its way to Scotland, 'Scots Guardsman' No 46115 comes over Shap summit in July 1965.

A fairly rare sight at St Pancras, No 46117 'Welsh Guardsman' takes the down Robin Hood Express to Nottingham.

# Scots in Service

As soon as the first of the Royal Scots became available for traffic, they were rostered on the more arduous duties on the West Coast route. Needless to say, the most important of these was the *Royal Scot* itself the prestige train of the railway. This ended the need to exchange locomotive at Carnforth, and eliminated the double heading that had been rife. By the end of 1927, a new wind was blowing through the LMS.

The company had every right to expect that an experienced firm of locomotive builders would supply a capable machine. The *Royal Scot* surpassed everyone's expectations – it was a brilliant locomotive. Aware of the importance of the new machines, Fowler arranged for the workings to be thoroughly studied, and so the dynamometer car came into regular use. This was the ex L&Y car, probably the best available in Britain at the time. E.S. Cox has recorded how, as a young engineer, he was frequently in charge and judging from his comments, he revelled in the opportunity of studying the performance of LMS locomotives on the road.

The results were remarkable, and in December 1927, at the Institution of Mechanical Engineers, Sir Henry Fowler took the opportunity to discuss the performance of the Royal Scots. This provided an unparalleled opportunity for some extra publicity, and so Sir Henry made sure that the results of the recent tests were widely known.

Only a few years before, the Institution had been stunned to learn of the low coal consumption of the Castle class, 2.83 lbs (1.28 kg) per hour per drawbar HP. The

*Royal Scot,* had from 31 October to 24 November recorded figures of 3.19, 2.94, 2.92, 3.32, 2.86 and 2.82 lbs per hour (1.45, 1.33, 1.32, 1.51, 1.30, 1.28 kg per hour).

Fowler however, qualified these remarks by mentioning that he had planned a Compound Pacific. He suggested that had it been built, it would probably have produced even better figures. But, as Sir Henry generously pointed out, not only were the new locomotives considerably simpler, they had also been put on the road just seven months after they had been designed – a remarkable achievement in itself.

The LMS, and Fowler, had their moment of glory. Unfortunately, however, the Horwich dynamometer car was somewhat out of adjustment, and the coal consumption per drawbar HP was actually slightly higher than the recorded figures. Luckily, higher consumption had no great significance, for coal was relatively cheap. What really mattered was that the trains were being handled with ease and, for the first time in well over a decade, the West Coast route was being run in a thoroughly effective fashion.

This is perhaps best illustrated by the test run of 23 November 1927. The train consisted of normal load, 15 coaches, plus the dynamometer car, a tare of just under 450 tons (452 tonnes). It was a fairly heavy load for a non-stop run from Euston to Carlisle on the Royal Scot express, especially when one considers that the passengers, their luggage and the parcels in the van added at least another 100 tons (102 tonnes) to the total. On route there were four permanent way slacks which slowed the train to a near walking pace. Two were on the run to Watford which the Royal Scot normally took fairly sedately; on more than one occasion, local trains headed by the sprightly Fowler 2-6-4 tanks would race the express to Willesden – and beat it! Nevertheless, the train took a fraction over 338 minutes to complete the 298.1 mile (479.7 km) run. The schedule allowed 345 minutes and this demonstrated the most important aspect of the new locomotives – they had the work well in hand. Nowadays, the student of locomotive practice and performance may dote on the logs of exceptional runs, but the operating staff had to take a totally different view. They needed a locomotive that could be relied upon to keep booked time regardless of the load, or of the conditions found along the route. Therefore a small, but significant margin had to be allowed to cope with the unexpected, and the

One of the Crewe-built Royal Scots, No 6154 *The Hussar* before the fitting of smoke deflectors.

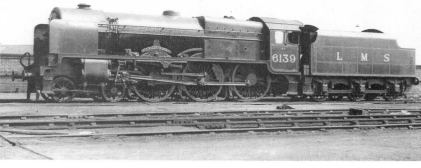

normal hazards of day-to-day running, like signal checks and permanent way slacks.

High performance was typical of the class as a whole, and the crews took to them with enthusiasm. Possibly, this was due to the machines' familiarity as many Midland features had been incorporated into the design. In 1930, the general success of the Royal Scots was celebrated when a further 20 were ordered, and built at Crewe making a total of 70 powerful machines for use on the whole system.

Although the boiler had many similarities with that of the Lord Nelson class, it differed in one significant feature. The Nelsons had a reputation for being shy steamers, a criticism no one ever levelled against a Royal Scot. The most probable explanation lies in two factors. Firstly, there were only 16 Nelsons, and these were spread around three divisions. This meant that the crews never had long to get into the feel of the machine. Normally, this would not have mattered, but for the dissimilarity of the firegrate. On other Southern locomotives, the grate had a single slope, whereas on the Nelsons it had a level portion in front followed by a slope. The Scots had the same arrangement, but there were 50 locomotives, so the crew on the top link had ample time to get to know their own machines. Furthermore, this particular type of grate was already well known on the route and the firemen were used to the tricks involved in maintaining an evenly burning fire. Southern locomen who praised the Nelsons always added the rejoinder that they needed sympathetic treatment, and that the fireman had to know his job.

The Scots were not without their faults. The most significant of these was the tendency for smoke to drift across the cab front. To some extent this was caused by the short chimney, but the main reason lay in the efficiency of the cylinders. Coal consumption was

kept to a minimum because it was possible to expand the steam fully before it reached the exhaust, whilst the power of the locomotive ensured that it was not necessary to thrash it hard. As a result, the Scot's exhaust was quite gentle compared to the violent pyrotechnics formerly associated with West Coast expresses, and the steam was only thrown a little clear of the locomotive.

The cure was relatively simple. In Germany, the same trouble had occurred a little earlier and had been solved by the addition of side plates beside the smokebox. These produced a sufficiently strong upward draught to carry the steam well clear of the cab. Eventually, simple, large rectangular side plates, echoing the shape of the firebox were adopted and the familiar appearance of the parallel boilered Scots was complete.

After a short time in service, coal consumption began to rise, not alarmingly, but sufficiently to cause concern. The main cause for anxiety was not the cost, but the need to be sure that the booked non-stop runs could be completed with sufficient coal left in the tender to provide an insurance against failure. There is nothing particularly clever in arriving at the end of the run with the fireman scraping the bottom of the bunker – only a short step away from the ultimate disaster of running short of steam a mile or so before the destination.

The cause of the slight increase in coal consumption was soon discovered. The long travel piston valves had a single wide ring to ensure steam tightness. When new, it was satisfactory, but after a while it began to allow live steam to leak directly into the exhaust. The ultimate cure was simple enough, the provision of a valve

Royal Scot No 6139, renamed *The Welch Regiment* in 1936, fitted with smoke deflector plates.

with a number of narrow rings. It was a solution that had cured the same trouble on the GWR a quarter of a century before.

Once the few minor weaknesses in the design had been attended to, the Royal Scots settled down to a decade of solid work on the LMS. The Railway's reputation grew; no other express passenger locomotive was capable of doing the sort of work regularly carried out by the Royal Scots.

As there were only 70 engines, more modern motive power was needed, and various ideas were put forward. Quite a few applied to the unfortunate Claughtons which never quite managed to do what was expected of them. After a larger boiler was tried, without success, the decision was made to reconstruct the lot.

All that remained of the originals in the first conversions were the driving wheels with their characteristic large circular centres. Even these disappeared after the first were built. The locomotives were pure accountant's rebuilds, that is they were charged to revenue rather than to capital and were treated as replacements for accountancy purposes.

The new design looked like a Royal Scot; it had the same cylinder arrangement, the same chassis and a substantially similar but smaller boiler. Unfortunately, the 'Patriots', or the 'Baby Scots' as many enthusiasts preferred to call them, were less effective than their big sisters. They were not exactly bad machines, particularly if one compared them to the Claughtons, but they did lack sparkle.

# Fury

In 1929, the North British Locomotive Co. built a 51st 4-6-0 for the LMS. The wheelbase corresponded to the Royal Scots and, in general outline, there was a family resemblance. However, No 6399, *Fury* was a completely different machine. Firstly, it was a four-cylinder compound, utilizing a super-high pressure boiler. Unfortunately, unlike the Royal Scots it was an ignominious failure.

In retrospect it is difficult to understand why the LMS chose such a complicated model. One can only suppose that the Superheater Co., British Agents for

the German Schmidt Superheater Co., were intoxicated by their own ingenuity, and managed to persuade the LMS to sponsor an experiment. They were ardently exploring a well known engineering dead-end, the fierce pursuit of thermal efficiency.

In thermodynamic terms the Stephenson pattern steam locomotive was a grossly inefficient beast. Its overall efficiency, based on coal burned against work done, was in the order of 6 to 7% maximum, 2-3% minimum. Every effort to improve its performance produced similar results; if the 'improved' locomotive managed to move at all, it broke down with monotonous regularity.

*Fury* was just such a machine. Its main weakness was the boiler and it is something of a mystery how the ingenious inventor managed to persuade anyone that it would work with any degree of

safety.

In place of a conventional firebox, *Fury* had a water-tube box which formed a complete closed circuit. To prevent corrosion of the tubes, the circuit was filled with distilled water and sealed. This working fluid was then heated to a point where its pressure was between 1,400 and 1,800 psi (95.2 bar to 122.4 bar). A heat exchanger was installed at the point where the normal crown of the firebox would have been and the closed circuit pipes generated steam at some 900 psi (41.6 bar). This steam went to the central pair of cylinders, which had 11½ inch (29.21 cm) bore by 26 inch (66.04 cm) stroke.

The exhaust from these cylinders was then mixed with steam at around 250 psi (17 bar) generated in the front barrel, which was a fairly conventional if somewhat short firetube boiler. This steam then went to a pair of

The LMSR three-cylinder high pressure compound No 6399 *Fury* as new at the North British Locomotive works in 1929.

The high pressure boiler and firebox for
No 6399 *Fury* being fitted.

18 inch × 26 inch (45.7 cm × 66.0 cm) Royal Scot pattern cylinders. It was a masterpiece of complexity. However, it did achieve something that many engineers regarded as highly desirable in the 1920s – it used extremely high pressure steam.

There was reason to believe that each development towards higher pressure was a step in the direction of greater efficiency. The main problem was one of safety for even at comparatively low pressures, a boiler had many of the attributes of an unexploded bomb. In addition, there was the problem of utilising ultra-high pressure steam in a working circuit. The Schmidt arrangement appeared to solve this dilemma by not using the highest pressure as anything but a heat exchange mechanism. This particular principle was very old indeed, and had been attempted before with a variety of fluids, all of which were believed to offer better heat exchange than water. However, there was one underlying fault. Although thermal efficiency was desirable, the touchstone of a locomotive's effectiveness was its commercial efficiency. Its purpose was to pull trains on time, preferably at an operating surplus, and the cost of coal, particularly before 1940, was not the major consideration.

The great virtue of the Stephenson pattern locomotive was its relative simplicity, although, through the century and a half of its life, various complications were added to the basic arrangements. Initially, it was modelled on the Liverpool & Manchester *Planet* 2-2-0. The *Planet* rather than the *Rocket* was the true progenitor of the steam locomotive. Despite the modifications it remained a very straightforward mechanism, which could be built reasonably cheaply. Furthermore it was not too difficult to maintain in good working order, even if it did burn a little more coal. British Railways bought coal by the wagonload at the pithead, and

usually managed to strike a very good bargain whilst so doing.

However *Fury* was a hostage to fortune. The boiler was a time bomb waiting to explode because of the introduction of the closed circuit firebox tubes. Indeed, bearing in mind the generally conservative outlook of Derby top brass, it is difficult to see why they didn't raise cain at the outset. Any locomotive man of standing must have known the sorry story of firebox tubes; they had been tried in various forms throughout the history of the locomotive boiler and until the development of reliable welding allowed the construction of the thermic syphon, they leaked like sieves. The function of a firebox was to oxidise material, and although the principal fuel was a mixture of solid hydrocarbons, one should remember that iron and steel can also oxidise. In the inferno of a locomotive firebox, they often did.

In this instance, the trouble was compounded by the introduction of extremely high pressure. This was essential in order to transfer heat into the heat exchanger, and to do so effectively enough to generate a pressure of 900 psi (416 bar), but it was a potentially dangerous business.

*Fury* began trials in January 1930. On 10 February 1930, one of the firebox tubes exploded. This was mainly due to the failure of natural circulation within the tubes, leading to local overheating and consequent weakening. At that pressure, very little weakening of the tubes could be tolerated. The Superheater Co.'s inspector, Louis Schofield, was killed outright, and fireman Blair was severely injured. Driver Hall and LMS Inspector Pepper escaped with shock. Some thirty years later, Inspector Pepper became assistant to the CME of British Railways.

The locomotive was laid aside, and was left at Derby for four years. No attempt was made to repair the firebox, so there it remained, unwanted and

dishonoured. Then W.A. Stanier took over the reins.

Stanier ordered a complete inspection, probably the only one made since the accident investigation. E.S. Cox states that Stanier had the boiler steamed, which implies that it had already been repaired. Stanier concluded that the boiler was a deathtrap and that the compound arrangement was probably not worth improving. Instead, a new central cylinder casting was fitted, and as the rest of the chassis was identical to the Royal Scot, this created the foundation for the 71st locomotive in the class.

However, instead of ordering that a spare Royal Scot boiler be put on the frames, he had it fitted with a new design of taper boiler. The result was renamed *British Legion* and numbered in with the Royal Scots.

To the enthusiast of the day, it was definitely an odd man out, a sort of enlarged and rather ungainly Jubilee. Part of the reason was the unusual raked-outside steampipes, which, whilst utilitarian, were hardly elegant. This feature was replaced by vertical pipes running into the rear of the smokebox. The nameplate was a replica of the British Legion badge, and to the writer, always looked vaguely like a skull when seen from a distance.

There was, however, one great improvement, for although *Fury* originally had a Fowler pattern 3,500 gallon (15,911 litres) tender, this clearly was replaced during the hibernation. *British Legion* received the high-sided Stanier 4,000 gallon (18,184 litres) pattern tender, and looked much better as a result.

*British Legion* was to become the pre-prototype of the 'Rebuilt Scots', the subject of our next chapter. However, it *was* not the first Rebuilt Scot, nor even a rebuild of a Scot, since *Fury* was originally an odd prototype machine, and not numbered in the Scot series.

# Stanier and the LMS

In October 1930, Sir Henry Fowler was appointed Assistant to the Vice-President for the works. His vast experience should, it was said, be devoted to research and development. Clearly, the board had had enough and the CME was being gently eased out, whilst being allowed to maintain face.

In his place, they appointed Ernest Lemon, the Carriage & Wagon Examiner. This may have seemed an odd choice, but one should remember that both Gresley and Churchward had spent part of their career in this field. Although the CME may influence the design, the actual detailed working out is done in the drawing office under the guidance of the chief draughtsman. Therefore, it was not absolutely necessary to appoint a man who was capable of designing a locomotive on his own. The cynic could also have pointed out that the LMS had been managing for almost 10 years with a CME who was not really interested in locomotive construction.

Superficially, the railway had been doing well enough, but this lack of direction was beginning to have its effect. There was one very considerable problem – the long standing differences of opinion between the three major constituents remained unresolved. Anything Derby did was bound to be opposed by Crewe and Cowlairs. Sir Josiah Stamp, President of the Company remarked later that if he had put a Crewe or a Cowlairs man in charge, then the other two works would have rebelled.

In retrospect, it is easy to see what should have been done. By 1924, each of the company's works should have been placed under a

fairly forceful and able man from one of the other constituents. R.A. Riddles, when faced with the same potential situation on British Railways, moved the senior men about and the results were generally good. However, by 1930, it was too late for this to take place on the LMS.

The Board turned towards Swindon. There, W.A. Stanier, second-in-command to C.B. Collett, was in a rather awkward position. According to GWR tradition, he could expect to succeed as CME, but as he was only a few years junior to his chief, his tenure of office would have been very short. It took some time to persuade Stanier to leave his secure, well ordered company, and take over an organisation he knew to be in a state of turmoil. Eventually Stanier took the hot seat and Ernest Lemon went on to do good work in the operating field.

Apart from the 60 Royal Scots, the LMS had a collection of 'Patriots', a good 2-6-4 tank, and a collection of Midland inspired locomotives which were undersized, underpowered and occasionally, verged on the antique. These looked impressive

enough especially to the enthusiast, who tends in his liking for locomotives to hark back to his boyhood and the traditional lines of the Midland locomotives were very agreeable. Similarly the heterogenous collection of locomotives of pre-group origin were equally pleasing to look upon. It was an altogether different matter when it came to getting them to pull a train, which, we must remember, is the object of the exercise!

It is often suggested that the Board only turned to an outsider in order to stop the warring factions and restore order. This is a gross over simplification. Firstly, the factions were not simply at war; in the absence of positive direction from above, various individuals were doing as they saw fit to improve matters.

Secondly the Board's requirements were quite explicit. They needed a man of wide experience, who was a sound and original engineer, a good administrator and someone who could lead and inspire a good team. Stanier was, undoubtedly, the best man available at the time especially as Oliver Bullied was still rather too young, and there was no one on the LMS of sufficient calibre to tackle the job.

W.A. Stanier took office in November 1931, with a clear

Nameplate as fitted to *Royal Scot* No 6100 and retained through rebuilding to date.

No 6100 (or 6152) as prepared for its visit to the USA in 1933. A 'cow-catcher' was also fitted.

directive – the size of the locomotive stock had to be reduced. This meant that the locomotives had to be worked more intensively and spend less time in the shops. It meant the end of the Midland ideal, as previously the principle had been to cosset locomotives, and treat them gently at all times.

Stanier ensured another break with tradition by shifting the centre of design work to London, away from any of the factories. He then settled down to deal with the major deficiencies in the collection.

Once again, the Royal Scots proved their worth. Considering the needs of the railway, they were a little too small but still capable of the work and once the unsatisfactory wide rings on the piston valves were replaced with a number of narrow ones, curing the problems of steam leakage as wear took place, they were good, sound, reliable locomotives. The main need was for a second-line passenger locomotive, a good mixed traffic machine and a heavy freight.

Apart from the odd group of 0-4-4 tanks which appeared under Stanier's name, but which were clearly the final fling of the Midland tradition, Stanier began by producing a small class of Pacifics, the 'Princess Royals'. These were intended to work through from Euston to Glasgow, something no previous locomotive had been able to do, as the size of the ashpan did not permit this. It is not generally appreciated that the main problem with the coal-burning locomotive was the disposal of the solid products of combustion and this, more than anything else, led to the eventual demise of the breed. This was just a foretaste, and those who had reviled the influence of Derby joined with those who had gloried in it by castigating the introduction of Swindon practices, including the use of prominent, taper boilers. Initially, these boilers were domeless, and together with low superheat, they were the order of the day. However, when the first of the Stanier 2-6-0s appeared with a Swindon pattern cover over the top feed, Stanier ordered its immediate removal. He was not going to insist on such matters as domeless boilers and low temperature superheat once it was realised that they were less than satisfactory. In short, the initial

Relegated to local duty, The *Royal Scot* on down fast at Cheddington near where the Great Train Robbery was to take place.

The *Royal Scot* with headboard, bell and nameplate on the up 'Lakes Express' near Bolton-le-Sands. A milk float is next to the locomotive.

Stanier locomotives were not an outstanding success.

The Royal Scots had one last taste of glory when it was arranged to send an LMS locomotive to North America. The occasion was the Chicago World Fair of 1933, and a complete train of modern stock was shipped out with the locomotive. It is difficult to see how this could have benefitted the LMS, but presumably as the GWR had done so well with the visit of *King George V,* it was felt that the LMS might be equally well served by a similar arrangement. Stanier was no stranger to this procedure for he had accompanied *King George V* on its trip to the USA.

However, it was impossible to push forward the construction of the new Pacifics and therefore the decision was taken to send a Royal Scot instead.

Actually, the decision was taken to send *The Royal Scot,* and this has led to a degree of controversy over the years. Some believe that a substitution may have taken place, and that No 6152 was sent in place of the original, which was undergoing repairs at the time. However, no records remain to prove that such a change did occur. After the extensive work

carried out on the locomotive, there was very little of the original 6100 (or 6152) left in the machine that travelled from Tilbury on 11 April 1933. There was a new boiler, the bogie had been replaced with a new Stanier inspired design, and, of course there were the new piston valves. Undoubtedly other parts had been replaced or extensively modified, and the overall appearance had changed, due to the prominent smoke deflectors. Once in America, a bell, headlamp and pilot (commonly miscalled a 'cowcatcher') were fitted to conform to US and Canadian requirements, and the locomotive was beautifully finished, with every possible bit of brightwork polished. Another important difference was the addition of a new roller-bearing six-wheeled tender, which was intended for the turbine powered Pacific 6202 and finally an extra nameplate was placed across the centre of the smokebox door. Although the train was intended as an exhibit for the Fair, it was scheduled to undertake tours of the continent as well – unlike *King George V* whose main line runs were almost an afterthought. The first tour began on 1 May and ended on 25 May, when the train arrived in Chicago. After the Fair on 11 October, it set off again and finally returned to Montreal at the end of November having covered

11,194 miles (18,014 km) over US and Canadian rails. Not one of the spares that were prudently carried was needed, proving once again, that the best way to avoid trouble is to prepare for it. However, the train itself suffered considerably from vandalism or, if we wish to be kind, the attention of that peculiar breed of souvenir hunter who believed that the best mementos are not merely stolen, but are wrenched from their settings as well.

On its return 6100 (or possibly a renumbered 6152) retained its bell and collected a new, massive nameplate recounting its exploits.

One significant change to the class took place during the early Stanier years. The 5XP class 4-6-0, the Jubilees, was designed to take a new pattern 4,000 gallon (15,141.6 litres) tender, with a 9 ton (9.14 tonnes) coal capacity, the first of the true 'Stanier' tenders. But it was felt that a better use could be made of these large, modern looking tenders and so they were exchanged for the low Fowler pattern ones carried by the Royal Scots, these going to the Jubilees.

As related in the last chapter, Stanier reconstructed the high pressure compound *Fury* into a taper boilered version of a Royal Scot. Although this was the only conversion undertaken at the time, it was a portent.

33

# The Rebuilt Scots

Stanier is justly renowned, and regarded as one of the truly great locomotive engineers of all time, and yet his initial designs had one endemic fault. He brought with him from Swindon many excellent ideas and one which was decidedly less than successful – a domeless boiler with low superheat. Although the GWR was performing wonders with just such a boiler, when translated on to the LMS it proved a severe disapointment.

Stanier realised the mistake and a new domed high superheat boiler was designed for the two classes most affected, the Jubilee and 'Black 5' 4–6–0s. With the better boiler, the mixed traffic class proved to be perfectly acceptable, but the Jubilees were still felt to be not quite all they might be in terms of power output and performance.

The next step was to have a considerable influence on the Royal Scots for in 1942 two Jubilees were fitted with new boilers. These were Nos 5735, *Comet* and 5736, *Phoenix*. With larger, better boilers, the pair were uprated to class 6, and in practice, became the equivalent of a Scot. *Comet* and *Phoenix* were, by any standards, superb machines.

In fact, the new boiler was an exceptionally good one, a very free-steaming, easily fired design which the footplate crews appreciated. But only these two Jubilees were altered, suggesting that the class was, despite its known failings, perfectly adequate for the work it was called upon to do.

Amateurs may have wondered why a locomotive known to be not quite as good as it might have been and which could have been transformed by a partial rebuild was allowed to soldier on. The answer was simple, cost effectiveness.

In the heyday of steam, the railway workshops were partially protected from the raw forces of economics. Even so they could not indulge in pure engineering for its own sake. Indeed, there were plenty of men in middle management and above who appreciated the full implications of the practical engineer's first rule of thumb; 'If it works, leave it alone!'

In practice, the Jubilees, with the high superheat, domed boilers, were very good second-line express locomotives. They might have lacked sparkle, they might have given less skilled crews some anxious moments, but they did their job well, and were comparatively modern trouble free machines.

The Royal Scots on the other hand, were much older and their boilers in particular were coming to the end of their economic lives. Replacements would have been made in any case and the accountants had made due financial provision for this to be done when necessary.

It would have been simple enough to have fitted new identical boilers to the class and to have left

Rebuilt Royal Scot No 6114 *Coldstream Guardsman* in LMS livery. Note the absence of a smoke deflector shield.

them much as they were, but the general design was giving rise to second thoughts. In particular, the large smokebox proved to be a source of trouble and annoyance. Ironically the design had been chosen in preference to the more modern drumhead pattern because Derby design staff considered that the latter would be difficult to keep airtight. In practice, the angle ring on the Scot boiler turned out to be a source of weakness. By 1940, most of the design staff on the LMS were sold on taper boilers with drumhead smokeboxes and it became obvious that to build more of the old design would be a ridiculous waste of time and valuable resources.

Ideas went even further. In the light of wartime austerity, serious consideration was given to rebuilding the Scots with two-cylinder drive; the cylinders were reaching the end of their working lives, having been bored out to the limit of the design in intervening overhauls.

LMS No 6157 *The Royal Artilleryman* on up express near Stafford shortly after rebuild.

Most overhauls and repairs of a steam locomotive left the machine more or less in one piece. But by the time it had been in service for around 20 years, a locomotive was sufficiently worn and strained to make a more thorough repair advisable. It would be stripped down to its component parts and, by the 1940s, checked by X-ray or ultrasonics for incipient flaws. Indeed, if it were not for the resources of the railway workshops, the older locomotive would have been scrapped and replaced. In retrospect one feels that this might have been a better solution since it would have given the designers a much better chance of incorporating the latest developments in locomotive engineering.

By the mid 1940s the Royal Scots had reached this turning-point in their careers. The LMS took a radical view and, rather than patch up the machines, they undertook a complete renewal. Some parts of the originals remained, notably the cab sides, but most were replaced. A new design was created, built around the new boiler and a redesigned

set of cylinders incorporating improved exhaust passages on the Chapelon pattern. There is little doubt that one reason for this step was the wartime ban on the construction of new express passenger locomotives. Technically, these new machines were reconstructions of the originals and therefore satisfied the regulations but allowed the LMS to acquire some much needed new passenger locomotives.

However, the alterations were carried out without much haste. Rebuilding began in 1943, with 6103 *Royal Scots Fusilier* and continued until 1955 when 46137 *The Prince of Wales' Volunteers (South Lancashire)* (now a British Railways locomotive) was converted, rebuilt, or replaced by a new locomotive, according to how one viewed the operation.

The new machines were completely modern, powerful locomotives and were destined to carry the LMR through to the end of steam, as we shall see in the next chapter. By 1940, major faults in the steam locomotives had been pinpointed. Many of these short-

Mixed LMS and BR numbering. Cab-end view of No 46111 *Royal Fusilier* in 1948.

comings had been discovered quite early in the days of steam and satisfactory cures produced. As a result, the Rebuilt Scots proved to be powerful, free running machines, slightly faster than the originals and decidedly better at handling both exceptional loadings and severe permanent way slacks. They were also extremely reliable. These features endeared them to the

Post-Nationalisation Royal Scot No 46103 *Royal Scots Fusilier* carries the LMS tender with a BR number on its way through Paignton.

footplatemen, the shed staff, the operating department and above all, to the knowledgeable traveller. Regardless of power classification, based on paper calculations, the rebuilt Scots were in practice only slightly behind a 'Duchess' as a motive power on principal express workings. Indeed, their main disadvantages compared to the Pacifics lay, not in power output, but in features endemic to 4-6-0s in general.

One was, of course, the relatively restricted ashpan. The apparent virtue of the trailing wheels of a Pacific or Atlantic lay in the larger firegrate that could be fitted. But the greatest advantage from the operating point of view was the larger, less restricted ashpan.

In these days of central heating, fewer people have the problem of ash disposal in the home. However those who have used solid fuel will appreciate that ash disposal is one of its major drawbacks. On the railways, it was not just a matter of getting rid of the stuff, it also had to be carried along during the run and could not be allowed to build up and so restrict the flow of primary air under the grate. Accordingly, although a Rebuilt Scot could have taken the Royal Scot to Glasgow, the longer runs were reserved for the Pacifics which had more room for the ash. Indeed, E.S. Cox claims that the LMS considered a 4-6-4 for these services, mainly to cope with the accumulation of ash on the run.

However, there were plenty of duties a Rebuilt Scot could handle with ease. Of these, the Manchester and Liverpool services were the most important, with the Irish Mail route to Holyhead a close third. The Midland main line also made some use of the Scots and it was not until the class 44 and 45 diesels took over the major trains that Pacifics began to appear on the shorter runs.

The other major fault of the rebuilt engines was a distinct tendency towards rough riding. This was exaggerated when stiffer side control on the bogie was introduced in the early 1930s after a derailment at Weaver Junction. These adjustments and detail modifications to the rear bearings and their side control went a long way towards mitigating the fault in a *new* locomotive. Alas, there was little that could be done to ease the problem when the locomotive was in need of attention.

However, these were minor blemishes; the rebuilt locomotives were excellent machines, and all round favourites. Perhaps some enthusiasts mourned the departure of the chunky parallel-boilered class, but that was pure sentimentality. A few runs behind a Rebuilt Scot soon put an end to any yearning for the past.

# The Final Years

By the late 1930s the first of the Stanier Pacifics started in service and the Royal Scots were no longer the principal trains on the West Coast route. Even so, it was to be well over a decade before the larger locomotives took over all the more prestigious workings. The Scots remained the backbone of the express fleet. Indeed, they were always to be found on the Manchester, Liverpool and Birmingham workings and the Midland route depended upon them. *The Royal Scot* itself saw the Pacifics in service, for when the train was sufficiently loaded, it was advisable to run the Edinburgh portion as a separate relief working, and this was handled by the Scots. Once more they showed that they had lost none of their brilliance over the years. Indeed,

Carrying the first BR logo, No 46156 *South Wales Borderer* on the Trent Valley line in 1951.

Stanier, had solved the problem of the valves and sundry other minor modifications had been made in the light of experience. Thus the Scot class regained all its early sparkle, and coped more than adequately with arduous duties.

During the last peace time years, all of Britain's railways took particular note of road competition. The use of cars had become more widespread and road coach services, had vastly improved. The railways no longer possessed an overwhelming advantage. As part of the LMS policy an 'On Time' campaign was attempted, with considerable success trying to impart to the operating staff the idea that timetables were not intended to be works of fiction.

One important aspect of this campaign was the introduction of 'Special Limit' services. These were important trains which had

tight timings and were to have their loads held firmly to presecribed limits. At least, that was the theory.

Practice was somewhat different. Let us take as an example, one working of the Up Mancunian, which had an upper limit of 415 tons (422 tonnes), but on this occasion, with 15 coaches, amounted to 466 tons (473 tonnes) tare, and over 500 tons (508 tonnes) gross. The locomotive was 6166 *London Rifle Brigade* and the start was marred by some severe permanent way slacks, which lost an estimated 2½ minutes. Nevertheless, the crew succeeded in making up most of this, and although the arrival was technically one minute late, it was doubtful if any of the passengers even noticed. It probably represents something near to the peak performance of the locomotives in their original condition, for an overall time of 172 minutes for this particular run under steam is very good indeed.

As mentioned earlier, the Scots were still used on the Edinburgh

In early British Railways livery, No 46163 *Civil Service Rifleman* in black near Crewe in 1949.

No 46110 *Grenadier Guardsman* in original form unrebuilt in down express near Tring in 1948.

No 46154 *The Hussar* with an up boat train near Stafford in 1952.

portion of the Royal Scot working. O.S. Nock has recorded just such a run in May 1939 when with a tare load of 339 tons (344 tonnes) , 6132 *The King's Regiment (Liverpool)* brought the up express from Carlisle to Euston in fractionally under the booked time. Some time was lost early in the run, although Shap itself was taken in style and by Tring all had been regained. What is perhaps more to the point, is that at Harrow, the train was eased, for the old Euston Station was even more awkward to get into and out of than its modern successor, and a train needed to be well on path to avoid the ignomy of a signal check around Camden. This was acceptable on a local train – just – but not on a prestige working. Part of an engineman's skill lay in so judging matters that his passengers were quite unaware he could have arrived

With smoke deflectors fitted, No 46166 *London Rifle Brigade* takes the up 'Merseyside Express' near Stafford in 1953.

sooner if only the road had been clear! Indeed, the log showed how the driver adjusted the booked timings to suit his convenience and the run demonstrated the true art of railway operation, to ensure that there is time in hand in order to be certain that the schedule is honoured.

All this came to an abrupt end when Britain went to war. One of the first things to go was the express passenger train as overall speeds were savagely cut back and austerity was the order of the day. Otherwise, the first year of war saw little obvious change and although some of the younger railwaymen went to the colours, as they had in 1914, there was a far greater appreciation of the importance of certain civilian jobs and railway service was declared a reserved occupation.

The original Scots battled on through the war years, growing grimier with time and finally succumbed to an unrelieved black livery. The external neglect was matched by a decline in the standards of internal maintenance, and even the leisurely wartime

schedules were rarely kept.

It was, as related in the previous chapter, during this time that the Scots were completely rebuilt and virtually turned into new locomotives. It would be pleasant to record that the timings were improved and indeed, one can discover cases where a keen crew did their best to put matters right. However, on the West Coast Route timetables were to become a fine example of comedy at its worst. This state of affairs was to continue for a long time. In the 1950s, timings from Euston to Manchester were technically faster than over the more scenic Midland route and yet anything less than a 45 minute delay was a cause for celebration. This was not the fault of the locomotives as is shown by their performance over the Midland line. With a rather more arduous route across the Peaks, the Scots performed well running virtually to time except in conditions of fog.

It would also be pleasant to record a return to more normal workings over the West Coast route once British Railways had

*Above*: In the Yorkshire Dales, No 46108 *Seaforth Highlander* takes a down express near Skipton.

*Right*: Once the LMS' fastest train, No 46111 *Royal Fusilier* brings the 'Mancunian' into Euston platform No 4 in its original graceful form.

*Below*: With mixed stock of livery, No 46159 *The Royal Air Force* takes a down express near Bushey in 1950.

*Above*: A Midland train, No 46113 *Cameronian* with the 'Thames-Clyde' Express in 1953.

*Left*: A down Birmingham express passing North Kenton (with GEC electric train on next platform) hauled by No 46124 *London Scottish*.

*Below*: Under the wires, No 46140 *The King's Royal Rifle Corps* with second BR logo on tender, enters Euston.

improved the maintenance of both locomotives and track. Alas, on the West Coast route a new hazard arose – electrification, and with permanent way slacks liberally scattered along the route the final years of the Scots on the Euston services were bedevilled by adverse conditions. However by this time not only were there more Pacifics available, but the influx of British Railways' steam, notably the Britannias, had finally displaced the Scots onto less glamorous workings. Here they showed that in their rebuilt condition they were still masters of their work and it was only the general lack of enterprise in timetabling the secondary and cross country services which prevented them from demonstrating that they were every bit as good as ever they were.

The end had to come however, and in 1962 withdrawal began. By then the class had been completely rebuilt and re-numbered by adding 40,000 to the original number. The melancholy distinction of being the first to go fell on 4600 *Royal Scot* which together with 46139 *The Welch Regiment* went in October of that year. The workings of steam on revenue services over the nationalised system, was almost over.

By the 1960s all of the Scots' former glory had disappeared. Some effort was made to keep a few locomotives clean and neat, but generally neither time nor money were wasted on equipment due for the scrapheap. Whilst many enthusiasts flocked to watch the last runs, others, the author included, turned aside. To one who knew the locomotives in their heyday it was far too poignant to watch their sad decline – dirty, leaking steam, the nameplates removed for sale to collectors, their crews began to anticipate the nice new shiny diesels and hoped against hope that nothing would break down, for by the end of 1955, maintenance had virtually ceased and when a steam locomotive failed it was finished.

The Scots did not disappear entirely. Sir Billy Butlin purchased 6100 and placed it and other locomotives on exhibition at his

The up Mancunian near Willesden, hauled by No 46122 *Royal Ulster Rifleman.*

holiday camps. There, it seemed, they were doomed to slow deterioration due to salty air and neglect once their initial attraction faded. The exploitation of a once-mighty machine proved to be something of a mistake, for there are few things more dead than a steam locomotive without fire in its box and water in its boiler.

Eventually these machines left their seaside sites and went to preservation groups, where they received the attention they deserved. *Royal Scot* was particularly fortunate in finding a home at the Bressingham Steam collection of Alan Bloom. The locomotive remains in the anachronous LMS red livery chosen by Sir Billy: purists bewail this, claiming that in its rebuilt condition it should not be in LMS red. However, when a man is prepared to meet the considerable cost of maintaining a steam locomotive, it is only fair that he should be allowed some say in how it should look.

# What's in a name

In the beginning locomotives had names. Indeed, if any of the early locomotives possessed numbers on their owner's books, these have not survived for the delectation of present-day industrial archaeologists and anyone who dubs 'Puffing Billy', Wylam Colliery No1, is justly derided. The practice of naming a locomotive continued the tradition that began with the stage coach, and that was no more than a land-based translation of a marine tradition that goes back as far as man can remember. Indeed, the GWR never let one of its broad gauge locomotives carry a number. That indignity was reserved for the standard gauge stock and assorted locomotives.

The LNWR was also a firm believer in the virtue of naming, but whereas the GWR began to install order by instituting class names, the Premier Line, despite occasionally indulging in a string of connected names, shunned any such restrictive practices.

Of the lines that went to make up the LMS, only the LNWR and Highland Railways added names to their locomotives. Indeed, the practice, still fairly widespread in the 1840s, fell into disfavour, and by 1923 only the LNW, GWR, Great Central, and Highland gave names as a matter of course, although the LBSCR kept up the practice in a fitful fashion.

It is probable that the LNWR supporters were particularly annoyed when the new Company adopted the Midland practice of annonymity. The situation became even more ironic when the LNER began to name all the new passenger classes, despite there being no tradition of naming on the GNR or North Eastern railways.

Of course, to the railwayman, the business of naming was quite pointless. Most enginemen preferred to use the number even if a locomotive had a name and the records only employed the number. Originally, all railways had a capital list, which began at one and ran consecutively. At least, that was the idea. Once locomotives were withdrawn, gaps appeared; when a locomotive was 'renewed' or, 'replaced' by a new machine which had been paid for out of revenue, it was supposed to take the original number. If the original locomotive was withdrawn completely then the process was simple enough, but often there was still a good deal of life left in the old engine and so it would be put on the duplicate list. This duplication might mean renumbering, but alternatively it could merely be indicated by underlining the duplicate number, or adding a zero in front of it. It was all very confusing, especially for the operating staff. So, the system of block numbering arose, and reached its apogee with the introduction of the TOPS system for diesel and electric locomotives.

In 1923, some railways had gone fully over to block numbering. The GWR was probably the best organised, with a forerunner of the TOPs system, using a four-digit number of the 00XX pattern. Few railways maintained a proper capital list, having overlaid an original listing with block numbering, as new constructions were allocated groups of numbers from the outset. Grouping brought about the end of the capital list system of numbering, for it proved impossible to bring together three or more company's lists into any sort or order. Ironically, the one grouped line where this might have been possible was the GWR – the one that had completely abandoned the arrangement!

Initially, class listing was not too obvious on the LMS, because many of the new constructions were numbered into the low hundreds, and even the adoption of a four-figure system made very little difference. The old lists were assimilated by the simple process of adding so many thousand to the initial number and consequently new locomotives had to fill in the gaps in the series, although a certain amount of renumbering of intrusive locomotives was undertaken.

However the LMS board did agree that it would be a good idea to name their magnificent new locomotives.

Engines 6125–6139 received names that had been carried by

Willesden Junction before its disappearance with an up express hauled by No 46151, *The Royal Horse Guardsman.*

BR No 46101 *Royal Scots Grey* heads a down express near Kenton.

Making smoke. No 46103 *Royal Scots Fusilier* with the Thames Clyde Express.

Over Shap without assistance, No 46165 *The Ranger* takes a Liverpool-Glasgow train of BR Mk. I stock.

earlier locomotives, mostly from Liverpool & Manchester and the Grand Junction. These engines also carried a plate engraved with a representation of the original locomotive mounted on the central splasher.

The other locomotives were named after regiments in the British Army. This was to become something of a habit, and most authorities agree that it was a very bad habit indeed. But it had its good points too, for example it provided a good opportunity for publicity at a naming ceremony, especially if representatives of the regiment could be persuaded to

attend and donate a pair of crests to surmount the nameplate.

Perhaps it was hoped that regular soldiers would feel some slight affinity to locomotives named after their regiment. However, although members of the armed forces were, and still are, assiduous users of the railways, once they have a leave pass and a travel warrant, they do not particularly care what pulls the train. As for those who served during the 1914 war the great majority looked back on their time in the trenches as seldom as possible.

Regimental names are apt to get more than a little involved, which was another reason for their unsuitability. Many of the Royal

Scots acquired elaborate nameplates as a result, especially once the names of the best-known regiments had been used.

For example in the 1930s the second batch of 20 Scots just about exhausted the names of the better known units. Indeed, this second batch included the names of regiments of the Royal Air Force, while the last two of the series became 6168, *The Girl Guide* and 6169, *The Boy Scout*. The naming ceremony of 6169 was enlivened by the appearance of Sir Henry Fowler in the uniform of the movement; even it he was not particularly interested in the locomotives, he believed strongly in Scouting!

It is worth pointing out that *Fury*

In April 1961, No 46122 takes a London to Manchester express past Macclesfield station, recently rebuilt.

Rebuilt Royal Scot No 46105 *Cameron Highlander* working over Shap with backing assistance.

The 10.55 Birmingham to Glasgow, hauled by No 46106 *Gordon Highlander* over Shap Fell without assistance.

In Ayrshire the 7.00 am Carlisle to Glasgow express is taken over Polquhap Summit by No 46105 *Cameron Highlander*.

In 1952 the 9.15 am Glasgow to Liverpool express is taken over Shap Fell by No 46146 *The Rifle Brigade*.

fell into the 'Early Locomotive' group, although doubtless, the name was chosen to emphasise the power of the high pressure system. Events proved it to be an unfortunate choice, and the reconstruction was more suitably named the *British Legion*.

Of course, names meant very little, except to train spotters. These existed in large numbers long before Ian Allen made life easier by publishing his 'ABCs' and founded a flourishing business. Nevertheless, names cost little and

added something special to the locomotive. If they increased interest in railways, then their cost was repaid, not merely in the extra business, but also in encouraging a steady stream of dedicated railwaymen.

In retrospect, the 1920s and 1930s produced very few inspired names and the LNER's penchant for racehorses produced some hilarious results, whilst the GWR's orderly, but highly predictable class names became rather monotonous in the end. It has

An easy load for No 46160 as it takes the down 'Lakes Express' over Tebay troughs in July 1962.

been left to present day British Rail to return to the system's origin and so the electric successors to the Royal Scots have as fine a collection of names as any that have run over British rails.

Entering Crewe, No 46115 *Scots Guardsman* with the 11.10 Euston to Barrow-in-Furness.

# Modelling Notes

From the outset, the Royal Scots were popular prototypes for the major manufacturers. Naturally, in the 1920s and 1930s the models were for O gauge, since OO was in its infancy when the class was introduced.

Hornby had on their lists a model they alledged to be the *Royal Scot*. In actual fact it was a rather good representation of one of the larger Nord de Glehn compound Atlantics and as a 4-4-2, bore little resemblance to the prototype. The same model was also offered as *Caerphilly Castle*, *Flying Scotsman* and *Lord Nelson* suggesting that someone in Binns Road believed few children could count the number of wheels!

Bassett-Lowke, on the other hand, offered a reasonably accurate model in their standard O gauge range, with, both clockwork and DC electric versions retailing at the same price, £3.15.0. This amount converted to the present day equivalent is nearer £100, since it represented rather more than the average take-home pay of a skilled worker. An AC version, which would work with Hornby, was also available, but cost slightly more, due to the greater complexity of the sequence reverse.

In 1938, Hornby introduced Hornby Dublo, the first reasonably accurate 4mm-scale system ever produced. Their LMS offering (which did not appear until after the war), was the unstreamlined 'Duchess', for by then the Scots were out of the limelight and it seemed unlikely that a model would ever be offered the public. However, after the collapse of Meccano Ltd., the dies and tools were acquired by G&R Wrenn, who re-introduced most of the locomotives, and announced the production of an original Royal Scot. This remained a pious

promise in the catalogue for many years and most enthusiasts never really expected it to materialise.

Then, two new firms, Airfix and Mainline (Palitoy) entered the ready-to-run 4mm-scale market and, to everyone's annoyance, both announced that their first express passenger locomotive would be a Rebuilt Scot. Eventually, both appeared and both were very fine models.

The Airfix model disappeared along with the company, but Mainline took their chassis and proceeded to permutate most LMS 4-6-0s onto that particular set-up and eventually produced both the taper and parallel boiler versions of the Royal Scots, with a choice of tenders. Their policy of selective release means that at any given moment, some versions are not officially on sale, but often examples of 'discontinued' versions can be found in the shops, whilst quite a few find their way onto the secondhand market.

Wrenn eventually produced

Saved from the hammer. No 46115 at Dinting Railway Centre awaits its final repaint.

After restoration, No 46100 The *Royal Scot* with head board, but without bell.

Preserved and repainted to original livery, No 6115 *Scots Guardsman* at Dinting Railway Centre.

*Below:* Fresh from preservation, No 6115 hauls 'The Pennine Way Express'.

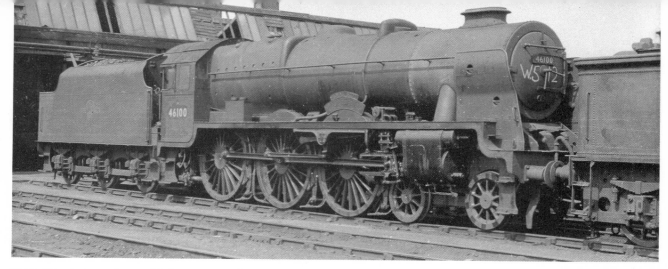

their die-cast version, which unfortunately lacks a little in detail and suffers from having the rivetted tender that was produced to accompany the Hornby Dublo 2-8-0.

A cast whitemetal kit is available from Wills Finecast for the unrebuilt version, but whether it is worth making up is debatable. It is designed to fit onto a Hornby (former Triang) chassis and is fairly expensive.

All the main LMS large passenger locomotives of the 1930s have now been produced in 4mm-scale and as a small selection of coaches are available, it is not unduly difficult to recreate the scene straight out of the box.

Some models are not 100% true-to-scale, but even the worst are far better than the pre-war Bassett-Lowke model and the best, in particular the Mainline 'Scots' are, if carefully built, collectors' items. The main point is, of course, that an enthusiast can set out to reproduce LMS and London Midland Region steam in 4mm-scale, knowing that he (or she) can obtain most rolling stock in ready-to-run form. As a further comment, it should be pointed out that, even at current prices, the Royal Scots of the 1980s cost less than half the equivalent price of the pre-war version, and are twice as accurate, and infinitely more detailed!

Mention should be made of the

Nearing the end No 46100 *Royal Scot* waits for withdrawal at Crewe.

large-scale Bassett-Lowke live steam Royal Scots. The design of the prototype, with its large straightforward boiler, made it particularly suited for this type of model. Initially, B-L offered a 3½ inch gauge version, but in 1939 they produced a 10¼ inch model as well. This last engine was a very powerful beast, and of the handful built, most saw good service on passenger carrying lines.

'Sans everything', *Royal Scot* without name or number awaits scrapping at Crewe in 1964.

# Royal Scot Names
# Numbers And Dates

| LMS No. | Name as built | Name from 1935/6 | Date built | Date reblt | With-drawn |
|---|---|---|---|---|---|
| 6100* | Royal Scot | | /27 | 6/50 | 10/62(a) |
| 6101 | Royal Scots Grey | | /27 | 11/45 | 9/63 |
| 6102* | Black Watch | | /27 | 10/49 | 12/62 |
| 6103 | Royal Scots Fusilier | | /27 | 6/43 | 12/62(b) |
| 6104 | Scottish Borderer | | /27 | 3/46 | 12/62 |
| 6105* | Cameron Highlander | | /27 | 3/48 | 12/62 |
| 6106* | Gordon Highlander | | /27 | 9/49 | 12/62 |
| 6107* | Argyle and Sutherland Highlander | | /27 | 2/50 | 12/62 |
| 6108 | Seaforth Highlander | | /27 | 8/43 | 1/63 |
| 6109 | Royal Engineer | | /27 | 7/43 | 12/62 |
| 6110* | Grenadier Guardsman | | /27 | 1/53 | 2/64 |
| 6111 | Royal Fusilier | | /27 | 10/47 | 10/63 |
| 6112 | Sherwood Forester | | /27 | 9/43 | 5/64 |
| 6113 | Cameronian | | /27 | 12/50 | 12/62 |
| 6114 | Coldstream Guardsman | | /27 | 6/46 | 10/63 |
| 6115 | Scots Guardsman | | /27 | 8/47 | 1/66(c) |
| 6116 | Irish Guardsman | | /27 | 8/44 | 9/63 |
| 6117 | Welsh Guardsman | | /27 | 12/43 | 11/62 |
| 6118 | Royal Welch Fusilier | | /27 | 12/46 | 6/64 |
| 6119 | Lancashire Fusilier | | /27 | 9/44 | 12/63 |
| 6120 | Royal Iniskilling Fusilier | | /27 | 11/44 | 7/63 |
| 6121 | H.L.I. (LMS period) | Highland Light Infantry: City of Glasgow Regiment | /27 | 8/46 | 12/62 |
| 6122 | Royal Ulster Rifleman | | /27 | 9/45 | 11/64 |
| 6123* | Royal Irish Fusilier | | /27 | 5/49 | 10/62 |
| 6124 | London Scottish | | /27 | 12/43 | 12/62 |
| 6125 | Lancashire Witch | 3rd Carabinier | /27 | 8/43 | 10/64 |
| 6126 | Sanspareil | Royal Army Service Corps | /27 | 6/45 | 10/63 |
| 6127 | Novelty | Old Contemptibles | /27 | 8/44 | 12/62 |
| 6128 | Meteor | The Lovat Scouts | /27 | 6/46 | 5/65 |
| 6129 | Comet | The Scottish Horse | /27 | 12/44 | 6/64 |
| 6130* | Liverpool | The West Yorkshire Regiment | /27 | 12/49 | 12/62 |
| 6131 | Planet | The Royal Warwickshire Regiment | /27 | 10/44 | 10/62 |
| 6132 | Phoenix | The Kings Regiment Liverpool | /27 | 4/48 | 2/64 |
| 6133 | Vulcan | The Green Howards | /27 | 7/44 | 2/63 |
| 6134* | Atlas | The Cheshire Regiment | /27 | 12/54 | 11/62 |
| 6135 | Samson | The East Lancashire Regiment | /27 | 1/47 | 9/48 |
| 6136* | Goliath | The Border Regiment | /27 | 3/50 | 4/64 |
| 6137* | Vesta | The Prince of Wales Volunteers (South Lancashire) | /27 | 3/35 | 10/64(d) |
| 6138 | Fury (Until 1929) | The London Irish Regiment | /27 | 6/44 | 2/63 |
| 6139 | Ajax | The Welch Regiment | /27 | 11/46 | 10/62 |
| 6140* | Hector | The Kings Royal Rifle Corps | /27 | 5/52 | 11/65 |
| 6141* | Caledonian | The North Staffordshire Regiment | /27 | 10/50 | 4/64 |
| 6142* | Lion | The York and Lancashire Regiment | /27 | 2/51 | 12/63 |

| | | | | | |
|---|---|---|---|---|---|
| 6143* | Mail | The South Staffordshire Regiment | /27 | 6/49 | 12/63 |
| 6144 | Ostrich | Honourable Artillery Company | /27 | 6/45 | 1/64 |
| 6145 | Condor | The Duke of Wellington's Regt. (West Riding) | /27 | 1/44 | 11/62 |
| 6146 | Jenny Lind | The Rifle Brigade | /27 | 10/43 | 11/62 |
| 6147 | Courier | The Northamptonshire Regiment | /27 | 9/46 | 11/62 |
| 6148* | Velocipede | The Manchester Regiment | /27 | 7/54 | 12/64 |
| 6149 | Lady of the Lake | The Middlesex Regiment | /27 | 4/45 | 9/63 |
| 6150 | The Life Guardsman | | /30 | 12/45 | 12/62 |
| 6151* | The Royal Horse Guardsman | | /30 | 4/53 | 12/62 |
| 6152 | The King's Dragoon Guardsman | | /30 | 8/45 | 4/65(e) |
| 6153* | The Royal Dragoon | | /30 | 8/49 | 12/62 |
| 6154* | The Hussar | | /30 | 3/48 | 11/62(f) |
| 6155* | The Lancer | | /30 | 8/50 | 12/64 |
| 6156* | The South Wales Borderer | | /30 | 5/54 | 10/64 |
| 6157 | The Royal Artilleryman | | /30 | 1/46 | 1/64 |
| 6158* | The Royal Regiment | | /30 | 9/52 | 11/63 |
| 6159 | The Royal Air Force | | /30 | 9/48 | 11/62 |
| 6160 | Queen Victoria's Rifleman | | /30 | 2/45 | 5/65 |
| 6161 | King's Own | | /30 | 10/46 | 11/62 |
| 6162* | Queen's Westminster Rifleman | | /30 | 1/48 | 6/64 |
| 6163 | Civil Service Rifleman | | /30 | 10/53 | 9/64 |
| 6164 | The Artist's Rifleman | | /30 | 6/51 | 12/62 |
| 6165 | The Ranger (12th London Regt.) | | /30 | 6/52 | 12/64 |
| 6166 | London Rifle Brigade | | /30 | 1/45 | 10/64 |
| 6167* | The Hertfordshire Regiment | | /30 | 12/48 | 4/64 |
| 6168 | The Girl Guide | | /30 | 4/46 | 5/64 |
| 6169 | The Boy Scout | | /30 | 5/46 | 7/63 |
| 6170 | Fury (as 6399) | British Legion | /29 | /35 | 11/62 |

Notes
\* Not rebuilt until in British Railways ownership

(a)  Originally 6152 until 1933. Preserved as LMS 6100 by Sir Billy Butlin. Now at Bressingham.
(b)  The first true rebuild.
(c)  Last of Class.
(d)  Original 6100 until 1933.
(e)  Withdrawn for rebuilding in 1947.

# Acknowledgments

The publishers would like to thank the following for their co-operation in supplying illustrations.
All colour photographs: Colour Rail

B/W photographs: Cecil J. Allen Collection, C. J. Freezer, John Marshall, National Railway Museum York, Ann Tilbury, R. M. Tufnell. Dr. W.A. Sharman

The *Royal Scot* after its rebuild in BR livery with post-American tour nameplate, but without headboard and bell.